EMERSON THE MAGNIFICENT!

Published by Christian Devotions Ministry, P.O. Box 6494,
Kingsport, TN, 37663
www.christiandevotions.us * books@christiandevotions.us

Published in association with Lighthouse Publishing of the
Carolinas.

Available direct from your local bookstore, online or from
the publisher at: books@christiandevotions.us

Printed in the United States of America

ISBN-13: 978-0-9822065-2-2
ISBN-10: 0-9822065-2-6
1. Christian life. 2. Spiritual life. 3. Devotions.

To the glory of God

EMERSON THE MAGNIFICENT!
How an old bike takes a young man for the ride of his life!

By
Dwight Ritter

"What do you have there in your hand?"
the Lord asked him.
And he replied, "A shepherd's rod."
"Throw it down on the ground,"
the Lord told him..
So he threw it down—and it became a
serpent, and Moses ran from it!
Then the Lord told him, "Grab it by the
tail!" He did, and it
became a rod in his hand again!
Exodus 4:2-4

Chapter One

Once, not long ago, there was an old man who
lived by the sea in a ramshackle frame house
with wooden shingles that were grayed and
rotting like old teeth from chewing tobacco—no
longer clean and sharp, but black and pitted.
One could never see inside the house because
the old man had pulled all the shades, leaving
windows with only blank stares. The doors to
the garage opened out like worn mule blinders.
One had begun to crumble and tilted perilously.
The house sat on a mound of sand surrounded
by other mounds—goose bumps on the

landscape.There was very little foliage, just
clusters of shiney eel grass and hardy beach
roses that would not die. No trees, sand instead.
Sand that could tell stories of generations of
the old man's family who played in the house,
dug clams from the flats with bleeding fingers,
ran over the dunes in reckless abandon, made
castles and dragons on the beach and swam
in the ocean when the tide was in. Often the
tide was so forgiving when it receded, that one
could almost see footprints from the past on the
flats like faded scratches of ancient thought on
pyramid walls.

Here the tide ebbed for two miles, and
when it was dead low, one could not see where
the ocean began, only brown and lilac colored
muddy sand, poking through shallow puddles.
Sprouts of eel grass that spent exactly half
their lives under twenty feet of salt water were
patrolled by strange looking horseshoe crabs,
ancient creatures like sci-fi tanks wandering the
depths guided by something that no one seemed
to know or care about. During the hot days of
August at low tide this huge tidal flat stretched
for two miles by twenty miles—an empty, hot

frying pan with eye-blinking mirages at the horizon.

Tom was the name of the old man who lived in the rundown house on the edge of these flats. Tom. He had spent so many years hiding in its dark interior that few citizens of the community knew much about him. Only rumors. No one visited him and he talked to very few people. He existed much like the house in which he lived, isolated and rundown; a sorespot in the community. And as families moved away from the community and new families replaced them, stories of those who no one saw regularly disappeared like lyrics to a song you used to know; forgotten histories, indecipherable initials carved in an old tree, an abandoned yearbook.

How old was Tom? No one could tell for certain. They could only guess when they saw him at the local grocery store buying Lucky Strikes cigarettes, Franco-American spaghetti in the can and tomato soup, white bread,strawberry preserves and peanut butter.

"He's gotta be late seventies," one would say. "No way," another would reply, "I'll bet he's ninety if he's a day."

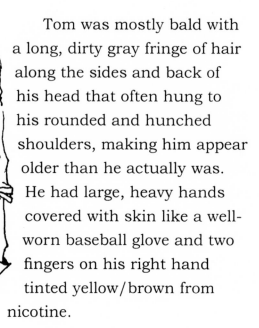

Tom was mostly bald with a long, dirty gray fringe of hair along the sides and back of his head that often hung to his rounded and hunched shoulders, making him appear older than he actually was. He had large, heavy hands covered with skin like a well-worn baseball glove and two fingers on his right hand tinted yellow/brown from nicotine.

Early each morning he walked to the grocery store, usually around six o'clock to avoid people, shuffling down the sandy road from his house with his hands jammed deep into his pockets, kicking a rock with his black Chuck Taylor sneakers.

Occasionally someone would try and strike up a conversation with Tom but with little success.

"Nice mornin',uh?" the grocery store owner said.

"Gonna be hotter'n blazes," Tom sneered. "I hate this time of year."

A clerk at the hardware store asked him his name. "Tom," he replied.

"Tom what?" the clerk asked in a friendly way.

"Just Tom. That's all," he said gathering the electrical outlet he purchased and leaving the store.

A local woman from the church visited him once and he told her to mind her own business. "Meddlin' old hen," he sputtered as she got into her car and drove away.

Chapter Two

Tom's house was built by his grandparents in the late 1870s out of wood and sweat and love. It was warm and inviting back then with climbing roses draped over the porch railings and fresh laundry blowing on the line like dancing butterflies. A charming breezeway with windows always open allowed the chickadees and wrens a place of refuge from the weather. Bird droppings on the counters and floor created a white-wash patina in the room.

Tom was born and raised in the Midwest. When he was six months old his mother brought him to meet his grandparents, a two-day train ride from their home. And so started an annual trek for Tom and his mother. When Tom was very young—four or five—his mother began leaving him with his grandparents for the entire summer. . . every summer of his young life, swimming in the ocean, digging clams for dinner, pulling lobster pots with his grandfather, and in the evening, listening to his grandmother read stories from a handmade storybook she had assembled over the years. Each page was a fabric patch cut to size with pinking shears. And glued to the fabric pages were carefully cut illustrations from old Bibles, *Harpers Weekly, The Saturday Evening Post* and other books and magazines. . . a hundred or so pages that showed the stories his grandmother would tell. There were no words in the storybook. They were in his grandmother's head, and they changed each time she read. Stories upon stories recited quietly each night while he sat mesmerized in his grandmother's lap, then drifting to sleep, breathing in the comfortable aromas of his grandmother's lavender sachet and his grandfather's pipe and the sound of an owl hooting and waves lapping on the sandy shore.

Because of the isolated location of the house Tom had no playmates. So when he was

eight years old his grandfather bought him
a new red Coleman Super Glider bicycle and
taught him how to care for it. It was a bigger job
than most people would imagine, because of the
sand and the salt air. Tom had to remove the
wheels from the bike every year when he arrived
and rinse the bearings in gasoline, then repack
them with axle grease and lovingly reassemble
the bike and wipe it clean.

He rode his bicycle on the hard salt flats
at low tide, dodging sharp-edged clams, and
then through the unpaved streets of town,
beneath the boughs of the large catalpa trees and
giant purple beeches.

He pretended he was a knight of the round table and his bicycle was his mighty steed. He named the bicycle Emerson—Emerson the Magnificent, and with the help of his grandparents he designed a family crest that was mounted on the handlebars. It was made much like his grandmother's storybook with small fabric swatches sewn on a background.

Libertadis, Strongalotis et Bravelaris was his motto. Sometimes Tom would carry a long lance topped with his family colors—purple and gold. The garage became the stable for Emerson the Magnificent, (the rigid shop broom was the stable groom). Oh what a life he led!

Tom was never lonely in the summer because his bicycle—strange as it might seem—could. . .

. . . well. . . it could speak.

Really.

It could converse with Tom, could teach Tom things that good friends teach each other. . . like how to open a pocket knife without cutting yourself or care and feeding of the breezeway chickadees. And because of Tom's youth and naiveté, he never questioned whether the bicycle spoke or not. It was no different than the birds greeting him in the morning, or his grandmother telling him she knew what he was thinking. Nothing out of the ordinary.

It was Emerson who said, "Watch out for the hole in the road," and Tom swerved to avoid it. Tom didn't know about the hole. If Emerson hadn't told him he would have plunged headfirst into it. So there was never any question about Emerson's real existence; no wonderment on the part of Tom at all. Clearly Emerson the Magnificent was an exceptional Coleman Super Glider!

Emerson told Tom they should carry groceries for the elderly, be polite to everyone and always be on the lookout for injustice. And they did, delivering capons from the duck farm, helping Mr. Graham spread seaweed on his vegetable garden, and never accepting any money. "If you accept money for helping the poor and needy," Emerson said, "you are diminishing the value of what you did. The value of serving others is measured by God, not by Mr. Graham."

Tom heard but didn't fully understand. Sort of the way a dog sits when his master says, "*sit*", but doesn't know why.

"Okay," was Tom's only comment.

Before the summer of his eighth year had passed, Tom told Emerson that he was his best friend, and at that age and bearing, Tom listened carefully when Emerson said, "You remember good friends—faithful friends—from your heart not your head. As you get older it will become harder for you to think from your heart. You will give in to your head and believe in logical things . . . things that make sense. When that happens you will no longer hear me."

Tom wasn't entirely sure what he meant, but he felt special having a friend like Emerson.

At the end of each summer Emerson would tell Tom the same thing (about thinking from one's heart), and each summer after Tom left, the message—though embedded—slowly dissolved like a tiny drop of color in a large glass of water. . .still there but unseen.

Over time, the fact that his bicycle actually talked to him also dissolved into a puzzling uncertainty.

Chapter Three

Tom's grandmother passed away during the winter just after his twelfth birthday. Only his mother returned for her funeral. The following summer Tom was sad. He missed her soft arms, her stories, the birdseed inside the breezeway windows, the laundry blowing on the line and the lavender smell of her undying love. Only a black and white photograph of her remained on his grandfather's dresser, smiling, her pale eyes —light blue Tom remembered—holding Tom's gaze. He would stand silently in front of the dresser inhaling and remembering.

"Why am I so sad?" he asked Emerson.

"Because you loved her deep within your heart."

That seemed too simple for Tom, and it didn't make him less sad.

Tom's grandfather let his wife go quietly. He was a solitary man who enjoyed being alone—with his wife, then by himself—sitting on his porch watching the ocean, toiling in his workshop no different than another silent tool, and smiling at his grandson which was worth a thousand words.

Emerson explained to Tom that his grandfather was not lonely. He preferred being alone. He was content with being in the presence of God. He missed his wife but he wasn't sad. So he kept busy. He sang tenor in the church choir. Tom could easily pick out his voice from all the other members of the choir. It wasn't because his voice was louder. It was because his voice was closer to Tom's heart, Emerson explained.

There were many messages from Emerson and his grandfather that Tom received in his early years. They rained on him like snowflakes in a windless white out. And like those snowflakes, they melted and disappeared too soon to remember, but staying long enough to taste.

Emerson told Tom about a bicycle he once knew. It was a Schwinn—beautiful in all aspects—shiney black, chrome headlight molded into the front fender, twin red sirens, colorful tassels hanging from the handlebars, a real leather seat with fringe, and elegant mudflaps adorned with chrome bullets. Gasp! It was as fast as the evening owl, making all other bicycles pale into insignificance. The only problems with this gorgeous bicycle were the brakes, the sprockets that engaged the chain and the bearings in the wheels; all those things that were under the surface but critical to the bike's performance. Over time the Schwinn began

to breakdown. The bike's owner, being more interested in the chrome and mudflaps, grew tired and impatient with its growing mechanical problems. Eventually that beautiful Schwinn ceased to be beautiful anymore. It became uncomfortable and unreliable, yet it was made to be ridden. So it became like a frayed clothesline that could never hold clothes. It could only be replaced with another new bicycle.

"If only that Schwinn's owner had paid attention to those things that make life meaningful, his bicycle would still be serving a purpose today," Emerson said one late-summer night just before Tom was to leave.

Tom thought he might buy mudflaps for Emerson when he returned.

Chapter Four

The summer of his seventeenth year, Tom showed up at his grandfather's house as he always did, but this year was different than other years. He had a pack of Lucky Strikes rolled into his T-shirt sleeve and he drove a 1936 Ford station wagon.

At first Emerson's heart skipped a beat when he met the car, like the feeling a mother has when meeting her son's first girlfriend—abandonment. Tom put him in a corner of the garage with his kickstand down (at the ready, Emerson suspected), and he stayed there, providing a safe home for spiders and mice. But he still was available for consultation. When Tom couldn't get the screw out of the oil pan to drain it, Emerson told him to use a five-eighths socket wrench. His grandfather had a new set in the garage. Emerson reminded Tom to change the oil frequently, check the air in his tires and especially test the strength of his brakes.

"How your car looks is not as important as how it runs," Emerson cautioned. "Remember the Schwinn!"

Tom did remember that bike with mudflaps and how beautiful Patti, who lived closer to town, swooned over that bike's owner. His thoughts were pulled to Patti and the gleaming Schwinn like sunflowers turning to the sun. It was Patti's pale blue eyes and curly hair (and the mudflaps) that were far more important than some hidden gears or grimy oil!

By the time he had returned to his home in the midwest, he was certain that Emerson's voice was just a figment of his imagination. Bicycles don't talk. It was like many things that we recall, things we might have made up. Like telling everyone we caught the last flyball in the ninth inning when we really didn't. But telling that story so many times and thinking about it, we begin to think it actually happened. Yet we know it didn't happen. Or do we? Obscured reality, or is it obscured fantasy? Do we want something to happen so badly that it happens?

When Tom left at the end of that summer, he said, "See ya, Emerson. I'll be back."

"Yes," Emerson replied, "I know."

Though Tom barely heard his voice.

Chapter Five

The United States Army drafted Tom one year later and he went to war. The memory of seeing the enemy frozen in the sites of his M1 rifle became permanently etched behind his eyes. He watched men in uniforms fall to the ground like soupcans shot off a fencepost. The reality that they were people, not soupcans, hit him a year later, hit him like awakening from a bad dream and finding it was real. A cold knife in his chest he couldn't remove. He never told anyone about the war but carried those memories like a painful sty that stung everytime he blinked.

He didn't visit his grandfather for many years after the war, summer vacation was over in Tom's life. He drove a truck, then he started his own trucking business. Before he was thirty he had married, had a son named Bill, went broke and started another trucking business.

When Tom thought back about his childhood, he was perplexed at his ingenuousness. . . a talking bicycle, an aromatic grandmother and a silent grandfather. How absurd!

The war taught Tom that he needed to be in charge of his life. Only *he* could control its outcome. "Counting on others can only get you get killed," he said. Tom had become an "adult". He had a family to provide for, food to put on the table, a mortgage to pay. Deep in the recesses of his cold, cold heart he had a fading memory of Emerson the Magnificent. And that stayed with him like keen eyesight; something helpful that was always there. Of *Libertadis, Strongalotis et Bravelaris!*

After his parents died in an automobile accident beside a snow swept Iowa cornfield, Tom felt compelled to return to the East and console his grandfather. He and his family drove for two days to visit his childhood "home away from home." It was cold during that winter and the wind howled through the window jams and shook the doors of the old house like a clumsy intruder. The beach was raw, gray and ugly and had accumulated large ice chunks, some taller than Tom. It was terribly uncomfortable and his wife and son couldn't wait to leave. "This is the most horrible, desolate place on the planet," his wife remarked. It seemed like wasted time from the past.

Tom sat on the porch with his grandfather, the icy wind swirling through their presence. They talked very little. His grandfather thanked him for coming with his eyes and said, "Come back, boy."

"I will," Tom whispered, looking out onto the angry ocean, knowing for certain this was the last time he would visit this fairyland.

Before leaving Tom checked out the old garage. There was emerson still propped against the wall. He thanked Tom for coming. Tom was shocked, perplexed, confused. The bicycle still seemed to talk. He knew it shouldn't. No one else heard it. Maybe it really didn't happen. Truly he was nuts, he thought as he slowly closed closed the garage door behind him, shaking his head, wondering.

Chapter Six

Tom's adult life always seemed to be a struggle, like a knot he couldn't untie. His trucking business was continually short of money. People were late paying him because he was too busy to get to his billing, and he didn't trust anyone else enough to hire them. Competition in the trucking business picked up and Tom began losing clients. There was a "network" of truckers who all enjoyed each other's company. Tom didn't trust them. He tried his best to make it work, but the business seemed meaner and angrier than Tom (and he was pretty angry at that point). Soon he owed money to everyone, especially the government who refused to understand his dilemma and sent him to jail for tax evasion.

After his release, jobs were difficult to come by. Then his wife left him and married the town mortician. His son, Bill, was ashamed of his father, so they spent little time together. Tom's life imploded: no money, no family, a prison record and no work.

He wondered why these things were happening to him. *Why didn't these things happen to others? What have I done wrong?* he wondered. *There are a lot of people much worse than me. How do they get away with it?*

A friend told him that he must reach out to God. "Pray your heart out, man" his friend said. "God is there. He's trying to get your attention. Turn your life over to Him."

Tom got down on his knees and prayed. He asked God for something good to happen to him. . .for some money, for his family to come back. He prayed for a sign, for a voice, for anything. He talked to the pastor of a local church who quoted some words from the Bible like "Ask and ye shall receive," but Tom didn't receive.

Life, he surmised, was a giant struggle—a war, and he had to win. He blamed God when things didn't go his way and asked God for a reason. The more he asked, the more nothing happened.

Finally he concluded that there really was no God. *If God is supposed to be a loving God, why does he do bad things to me? It just doesn't make a lick of sense.*

The pastor, unable to pass on words that made any sense to Tom, gave him a beautiful pastel-colored book mark. This was written on it:

If there is no God, why is there so much good?
If there is a God why is there so much evil?
                    Augustine

Tom never read it. *Why bother,* he thought. If the solution to all of his problems was a pastel-colored bookmark, this God thing was not going to be for him. *Senseless theories drummed up several thousands of years ago are not my cup of tea.*

As soon as he came to that conclusion good things began happening. He got a steady job driving a large eighteen wheeler from coast to coast. That was fine because he didn't really have roots. . .no place to go. The pay was good and the money he didn't spend on the 3 "W"s (whiskey, women and what-not), he put away.

"Some people don't need God," he said, cautiously at first, then with conviction.

According to Tom, the next good thing that happened was that his grandfather died, leaving him the old house on the water and enough money so Tom didn't have to work at all, only if he needed something special. Tom didn't need anything special except a little whiskey from time to time and a fresh pack of Lucky Strikes.

God would never have done this for me, he thought, standing in his front yard looking out over the dunes and onto the crisp blue water of the bay. *This—all of this—is just good luck! All God ever did for me was to let me down. People with money don't need a God. God is for the not-too-smart, for people who have no luck. God is an excuse man uses when nothing is going right. Trust in the Lord, the foolish people say.*

And that philosophy formulated Tom's belief for many years thereafter. Emerson was stored in the back of the garage. He was silent from then on, but thought, *Pity the man that falls and has no one to pick him up.*

Then. . .

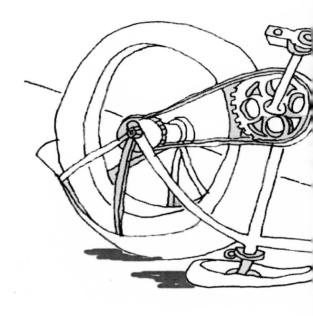

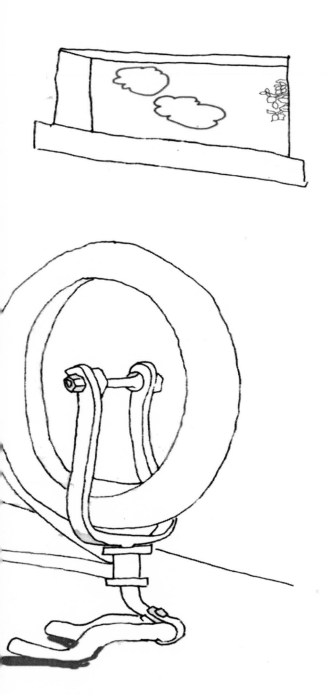

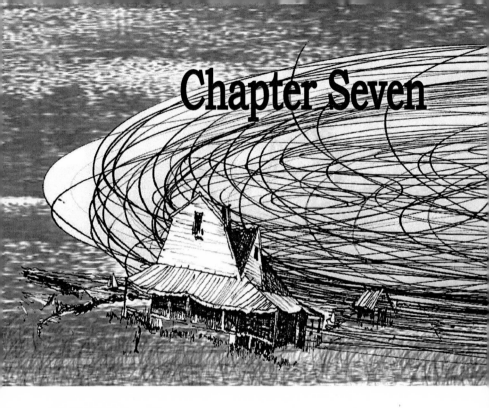

Chapter Seven

During the fall several years later a giant
hurricane swept up the coast like a raging beast,
howling and destroying. It was a surprise storm,
and caught the community totally unaware.
Unwisely, Tom was thrilled with the wind
and hail and the large waves. He didn't know
the difference between a fall nor'easter and a
major hurricane until it was too late. So as the
mighty storm approached, Tom stood atop a
nearby dune, leaning into the wind, feeling the
immensity, the low gutteral roar of the giant
tempest lurching in frenzy as it tore the coast
apart.

Suddenly this violent spectacle ripped
over the once peaceful bay like a giant swirling
demon, throwing Tom headlong against the
rickety old garage which shuddered and gave
a portion of itself to the storm. And the lights
went out as the tops of the dunes blew over and
buried the remains of the garage and Tom. And
there seemed to be a half a continent of rubble
blown in from the sea, scattered all around,
leaving no trace of that part of the garage or
Tom.

As suddenly as the storm came it left, and
the quiet was deafening. Everything was waiting,

unsure of the safety. Then some sand fleas scurried, an opossum lumbered over the rubble of the garage wall under which Tom lay and sniffed loudly.

A small whisper awoke Tom. It said, "Do not be afraid." But Tom's body was buried beneath the debris from the storm. It was claustrophobic under the wreckage.

"Urumph," he grunted, wondering where the voice came from. He tried to move his head under the oppressive weight but couldn't.

He heard the faint whisper again. It said, "I will restore you and set you free."

Can't move and I hear voices. Tom put two and two together; he was dead, but he thought death didn't hurt unless of course he was in— he paused because he didn't want to think it— unless he was in HELL! He squinted his eyes, thinking he should open them but there was only the faint glow of tan/white sand. No, he wasn't dead. It was worse. He was buried alive!

"Calm your soul," the small voice said.

"I don't know what you're talking about," Tom uttered between pursed lips so he wouldn't eat sand. "Who are you?"

There was a long period of silence, just long enough for Tom to begin thinking he didn't really hear a voice afterall.

Then, "I am with you," the voice said as faint as the last "hello" of an echo. It repeated, "I AM WITH YOU."

"Then you better start digging to get me out of this mess." Tom said, frustrated.

And then from nearby came a familiar voice. "Get your knees under yourself and stand up." It was the voice of Emerson ... Emerson the Magnificent. "I hope you're all right," Emerson went on cheerfully.

As Tom pushed himself up from the rubble, sand, a few old shingles and a rake cascaded from his body. And there he stood, somehow holding Emerson by the handlebars.

"How'd I do that?" Tom blurted.

"I don't know, but I certainly am grateful. My spokes were caught in a lobster pot and my chain was broken."

Suddenly Tom realized he was once again talking to his bicycle and it brought back memories of happiness. . . of the knights of the roundtable and bicycling on the flats and caroming through the Pitch Pines at a hundred miles an hour . . . of *Libertadis, Strongalotis et Bravelaris*. Then his thoughts evolved into the frustration and unhappiness of the rest of his life, much like an old song that bodes of something bad . . . "Heartbreak Hotel", "Since I Lost my Baby", "Runaround Sue", and sadness renewed its grip on his chest.

"Tide should be dead low," Emerson said, cheerfully. "Let's see what kind of treasures washed ashore.

Tom kept squinting at his ancient bicycle. It seemed like he was a familiar character from an old comic book. None of it was real or permanent, only temporary like a play. He couldn't understand how the bicycle could be rideable, much less talkable, after so long. But there was air in his tires, a chain on the sprockets and the handlebars were straight. And then there was Tom, himself, uninjured after being, buried alive and maybe left for dead. And where was the voice that spoke in calming words.

The voice.

It was not logical.

"Let's go." Emerson exclaimed brilliantly, as only a bicycle can. "Tomorrow we can worry about the house and garage."

Tom hesitated only a moment longer before throwing a sandy leg across the bar. Together they raced down the pathway from the house, over the dunes, onto the beach, and atop the flats. It looked like nothing Tom had ever seen . . . like the deserted battleground of some war-torn area. Large piles of seaweed were everywhere held in place by wood scraps, doors, windows, a large dock from Bayside Lobsters and boxes and beds floating in the eddys. Pleasure boats that appeared to have escaped from captivity were leaning casually, waiting to be rescued by the incoming tide. And throughout the area there was an eerie silence filtering through the crystal clear air. "Yahoo!" Emerson yelled as they skimmed over the flats and shallow pools dodging the floating debris like slalom skiers.

Chapter Eight

At about the third shallow eddy, Tom began thinking how lucky he was to have survived. He began calculating the insurance he would receive in order to replace the garage. The house, too, must have been damaged and he realized he could receive an even larger insurance settlement, one that he could put into fast-growing stocks or bonds. Then he could sell the land and move to an apartment somewhere warm like Miami and live like a king. "Beachfront property can be worth a fortune!" he whispered. "First I'll get the insurance money then I'll put the property up for sale, as is."

Suddenly Emerson's front tire hit a long wooden plank. It snapped up out of the water and hit Tom square in the head, knocking him off Emerson and face down into a muddy flat.

"Tom," Emerson's concerned voice said, arousing him from unconsciousness. "Wake up. The tide is dead low. There's miles to go, treasures galore!"

"I don't wanna go anywhere, you stupid bike," Tom said, his forehead red and bleeding

and his nose listing sideways. "I'm goin'
home. Everytime I listen to you something bad
happens." He spit out a tooth and put his face
back into the cool mud.

"Tom, why do you blame everything bad
that happens to you on me?'

"You're just bad luck," Tom said through
the soothing sand and salt water. "And I know
bad luck."

"Sounds like you're a real authority on it."

"You bet I am. And I'm no dummy. It's
time I started thinking about me, not that
rundown house and especially a stupid talking
bicycle."

"Tom, I talk because you listen. And
because you listen, you believe."

"I don't believe in nothin'!" he screamed,
pounding the water with his fist. "N-O-T-H-I-
N-G!"

"Then why do you keep talking to me?"

It was quiet on the flats, so quiet one
could hear the tide rising, like a celestial exhale.
Tom had to force himself onto his knees because
the tide was coming in and he couldn't lay face
down anymore, too deep. His nose was still

bleeding and the salt and sand had become
embedded in the gash on his forehead. It stung
like cheap soap. A towel floated by and a hoarse
gull swooped low and landed, half waddling and
then swimming, looking for food in the drifting
pools of wreckage and trash.

Tom tried to right himself, but the pain
in his head wouldn't go away and forced him
back into the water on his hands and knees. A
slow current rinsed by him. He watched seaweed
drift by entangled in algae, cigarette packages
and a White Castle hamburger wrapper. A small
hermit crab scurried over his hand. Tom wasn't
thinking clearly. His mind was exhausted, more
exhausted than arguing with his ex wife. It
felt good to just crawl around in the water with
his head down, watching the blood drip off
his nose and into the water, diluting, swirling
and disappearing. Soon the rising tide made it
impossible to crawl so he sat chest high in the
water. Just an old man sitting in shallow water
two miles from shore. A book floated by opened
to a page. It was the Bible. A verse stood out.

"The Lord said, 'Go out, for the Lord is
about to pass by.' Then a great and powerful

wind tore the mountains apart, but the Lord was not in the wind. After the wind there was an earthquake. After the earthquake came a fire. But the Lord was not in the fire. And after the fire came a gentile whisper. 'Why are you here?'"

Tom sat in the water reading the phrase from the Bible and watching the water rise all around him. He could see the shoreline off in the distance.

"Sure ain't no Lord out here," he said, watching a door and two shutters float by with the incoming tide. "Just a lot of mess." He stood up because the tide was now higher than his chin. "No sir," he said tossing the Bible back into the water and watching the tide accept it. "No God in his right mind would pull a stunt like this. This was just a mighty hurricane." He breathed and became hypnotized by the heavy quiet, the exhale, the current as it whooshed by, a plover in flight whistling queet, queet, two terns making hollow sounding noises like killick, killick as they dipped within an inch of the water, shooting toward land. Just whoosh, queet, queet, killick, killick. Mezmerizing sounds in a vacuum. "No God. Just a hurricane." No echo. Whoosh, queet, queet, killick, killick. "NO GOD PERIOD!"

Tom looked back toward the land. It was a speck on the horizon. Even standing, the water was chest deep and coming in too fast. And Tom became afraid. His pulse quickened as he tried to run. . .running in water up to his chest. He could not move faster than the rising tide and the thought of swimming two miles to shore was horrifying to him. All he could do was call out, "Help!" yet his voice rang dead, traveling no further than his lips. There was no one to be seen, no one to help an angry old man stranded in the water two miles from the shore. Then a low floating telephone pole hooked his trouser leg and began unemotionally pulling him under the water.

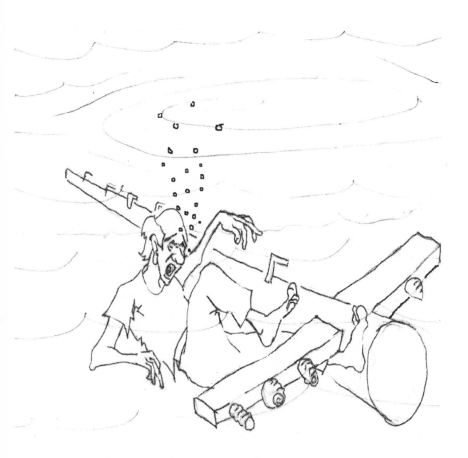

Come with me, it seemed to say.

"Help!" Tom called again desperately.

No one heard him. Only whoosh, queet, queet, killick, killick. The water surged suddenly into his ears, and startled, he gasped, inhaling the cool salty ocean. He looked up and the light turned to dark. Tom now belonged to the water-logged telephone pole beneath the water's surface.

You are mine, it seemed to say.

Help, he pleaded in his mind. *Lord, help me!* ""Lordle, hebelfelp!" he screamed into the water and coughed, inhaling for the last time.

"What is in your hand?" a whisper within his mind asked.

Tom tightened his hand and opened his eyes. It was difficult to see anything but he could make out a red, metal shape. It was Emerson. Emerson was in his hand, practically dead. He squeezed the old bicycle's handlebars.

"Now go home." The voice said, filling Tom with life. "There is much to do and little time to do it."

Who's voice is that? Tom wondered as his body left the telephone pole. My voice? Did I make that up, or is that the voice of God? And from beneath the water Tom cried out from his heart: "Here I am Lord! Here I am!"

Chapter Nine

It was still morning. The sun was huge,
flattened and reddish orange against the icy blue
sky. It was now just over the horizon beginning
its journey across the sky. The tide was surging
landward. And the strangest site no one would
ever see was making its way across the water's
surface.

"Libertadis, Strongalotis et Bravelaris!"
Tom screamed from the saddle of Emerson the
Magnificent. With his head back, looking high
and his wispy gray hair swirling around him,
he rejoiced. "Ahh! Great God. Wonderful maker.
Here I am!"

"Whoosh, queet, queet, killick, killick," the tide and birds responded.

"Onward!" Emerson shouted as they sped on top of the water like a skipping stone in ceaseless flight. "Onward."

And during this two mile bicycle ride atop the water, Tom never once thought that it wasn't happening or that it was even strange that an old man was riding a bicycle on the surface of the ocean. It was like being given a new heart, one that beat with a power greater than he could imagine. Now his heart ruled!

Once on the beach Emerson's tires sunk to their axles and their forward progress stopped, leaving them mired in the soft wet sand, fully upright.

"Let me help you out of the sand, Emerson," Tom said, pulling the old red bicycle up and onto the beach's surface. "You've got a nasty amount of sand in your chain, and I'll bet your bearings are a mess. Let's see if I can get into the garage and get you fixed up."

He carried Emerson up the dunes to his house. At first he couldn't find the garage, the dunes had shifted because of the strength of the wind, and the sand had piled as high as the roof. But there was no roof, at least not on the garage. It had been blown off and leaned against a clump of scrub pines and beach roses like a downed kite twenty feet away.

The house, though, was in better shape. It had seen several hurricanes in its life, some worse than this one. Tom shook his head. "Good ole place," he said, feeling a sense of belonging to the old family home.

After lowering himself and Emerson into the garage, Tom cleaned Emerson's axles and repacked the bearings in axle grease. Then he shined all the chrome until he could see the bent reflection of his face.

"Just like new," he said admiring the fine job.

"I feel like a new bicycle," Emerson beamed.

Tom worked quietly, straightening out the chaos in the roofless garage. Emerson sensed something was on his mind.

"What's up?" he asked.

"Are you God?" Tom said.

"Are you crazy? I'm a Colman Super Glider," Emerson answered.

"I'm serious," Tom probed.

"Tom, I am as surprised that you listen, as you are that I talk."

"There's more to this than that." Tom persisted, wagging a finger at Emerson.

"I am not God, Tom." A slow moving breeze whooshed by. Emerson continued, "I am the voice of faith that resides in your heart—still. I am the warmth of love, the kindness you feel for something small, the gentleness of a morning breeze, the tears of joy that you have yet to shed."

Tom shoveled sand from the door and re hung tools, glancing suspiciously at his bicycle. "Do all Colman Super Gliders talk?"

"Only if someone desperately needs to listen."

Tom quietly returned to repairing the workbench. "But all these things that happened—the hurricane ..."

"I had nothing to do with that."

"... my drowning ..."

"I had no idea."

"The voice in my head ..."

"What voice?"

"And you and I riding on top of the water."

Emerson turned his handlebars shyly. "Well, I will take credit for that."

"Why is God doing all this?"

"Because He loves you, and you are part of His special plan. God's been reaching out to you for as long I can remember."

"For as long as I first heard your voice?" Tom asked.

"Probably. And you've been trying to make sense out of it. God doesn't make sense to us."

"I'll say."

"His way is the mystery of the universe. It's as unimaginable as you and me talking to each other. If you tell people you talk to a bicycle, they're not going to believe anything you say. Humans only understand one dimension and one time span. God, though, is huge, ever present and forever. He works in miraculous ways only if you let Him.

"Do you understand Him?"

"I'm just a bicycle." He thought for a minute, his pedals rotating busily. "But because of that, I might be closer to understanding Him than you. Like most humans your faith has always been based on logic. You pray for money, you expect money. You pray for healing, you expect healing. God wants you to have everything you ask for, but he might deliver what you ask for shrouded in layers of time and readiness. There is no human logic to it."

"Like hearing with your heart not your head." Tom volunteered.

"You remember."

"I do, but *layers of time and readiness*?"

"Uhm. I was worried about that part."

Tom was antsy. No time to deal with abstracts. "Let's go check out the house. I clearly forgot about it."

Chapter Ten

It was afternoon of the day of the great hurricane. The sky was so clear it seemed to tingle with freshness. Chickadees rejoiced as they scampered over pine cones still attached to the scrub pines, buffeted from the winds.

"Smell that air," Tom said filling his chest with crisp, ripe air, the kind of air that fills your heart with eagerness and anticipation. "I remember this smell from when I was a boy. My grandfather used to say that country air weighed considerably less than city air. I never questioned him." "I remember," Emerson said.

"You were there?"

"If you were."

He and Emerson made their way to the house. It was still alive, Tom noticed. Shutters half hanging and swaying in the glistening sunlight as if impatient. The front door was open, welcoming them both. Many windows were broken and curtains dangled outside like careless shirttails.

A loud scurry and a bang from the bedroom caught Tom's attention. He cautiously approached the door and opened it a crack. Inside was a fox. Its back leg had become entangled in a wire from a large standing room lamp. He had obviously tried to escape, pulling the lamp over and getting it stuck under the legs of the bed. The fox was trapped and faced his enemy with courage.

"Easy there, fella," Tom said, squatting down trying to soothe the animal.

The fox ran under the bed against the wall and growled.

Tom lay down and looked under the bed. "Nice fox. I'm not gonna hurt you, but I've got to set you free." Compassionately he reached his hand slowly toward the fox, but the fox lunged at Tom almost biting him.

"Well that's not going to work. Sorry, Mr. Fox, but I have to set you free or shoot you."

Tom decided he would move the bed away from the fox, then maybe he could feed it and befriend it. Slowly he dragged the mattress and blankets off the bed. The fox, filled with hatred and fear, glowered and snarled.

"I dunno, Mr. Fox. You don't look any too grateful for my help."

Tom raised up the bed frame to untangle the lamp from the bed legs. The fox leaped at Tom's leg grabbing him by the ankle.

"Ouch! NO! Stop it! Leggo!" Tom yelled, kicking the fox in the head with his other foot. The fox raced out of the bedroom door dragging the lamp until it became snagged in the doorway. Then the wire broke and the fox ran, limping out of the house, dragging the lamp cord behind him.

"Goodbye, Mr. Fox," Emerson said cheerfully.

"Why are you so happy? That animal dang near chewed my leg off!" Tom shrieked.

"I know. What a timely event."

"What are you talking about?" Tom said, attempting to put his foot in the kitchen sink and run water over the bites.

"God just explained 'shrouded in layers of time and readiness' to you."

"Ough," Tom grimaced in pain as he covered his wounds with rags.

"You felt sorry for the fox so you showed compassion. But the fox didn't understand, did he?"

"Not at all."

"The fox saw you as the enemy. He watched you throw things in rage. He hated you."

"I wasn't throwing things around in a rage."

"The fox didn't know that. He thinks differently than you. He thinks you're trying to kill him. But you can't walk away and leave him or shoot him because you're a compassionate human. So you lift this huge bed up like you're going to kill him with it."

"I wasn't going to kill him! You sound like my ex-wife."

"I know you weren't going to kill him. But the fox didn't understand. You were being compassionate."

"Painfully compassionate, yes."

"The poor fox thought you were being cruel. He reached this incorrect conclusion because he is not a human . . . doesn't think the way you think. Humans reach similar incorrect conclusions about God because humans are not God."

Tom dabbed his wounds some more and thought about a lifetime of misunderstanding God; of asking for red and getting green, of wanting good and getting bad, and feeling good about doing bad.

Emerson continued, "God acts similarly with humans. You can't understand why He seems to hurt you. You can't understand the motivations of God any better than the fox can understand the motivations of you."

"It still hurts like crazy and look at the mess!" They looked around the bedroom. The floor lamp was laying on its side halfway out the door. The shade was ripped and shredded. The dresser layed askew against the bed stool.

His grandmother's picture had fallen on the floor, breaking the glass. Also his grandmother's favorite vase was broken. . . the large blue vase that sat on the dresser for as long as Tom could remember, broken into a million pieces.

"Look at this," Tom said, picking up from the broken pieces, the old fabric book she used to read to him, and also there was her lavender sachet, still alive. He inhaled the aroma of her memory and felt her love re-enter his heart. "How wonderful. How absolutely wonderful."

He stood in the shambles of the bedroom thumbing through the cloth pages of his early life, recalling the softness of his grandmother's voice and the silent wisdom of his grandfather.

"Layers of time and readiness," Emerson mused.

Chapter Eleven

During the week it took to dig out the garage, replace the roof and repair the house a fire truck came down the sandy driveway, its red light flashing heroically. Tom went out to greet him because the driveway was filled with wet, soft sand and the fire truck would surely become stuck.

"Good morning," the fireman said. "Are you alright?"

"Couldn't be better, but I could use some electricity," Tom replied.

"Another couple of days and we should get you hooked up. Doesn't look like you got a lot of damage," the fireman said, looking around the property.

"My garage was the worst. Everything else was minor."

Then Emerson said, "Excuse me, Mr. Fireman but was anyone seriously hurt?"

"If you need anything, just call." The fireman said, as if he heard nothing.

Tom thought it was strange that the fireman didn't answer Emerson. So he repeated the question. "Was anyone seriously hurt?"

"Yes sir. Sorrowfully we lost Frank Kynor and his wife, Bennet, when a tree fell over on their house; big old dutch elm, it was. Must a been a hunnerd years old. Fell right through the roof and landed on 'em both whilst they was in bed. Horrible. I seen 'em. Oowee! Then the Bickell's son Jack—don't know if you ever knowed him—well he was hit with some flyin' debris and he never recovered. Yep. And ole Bif Stewart went down to the beach to tie up his boat,and we ain't seen him since. Lot's of folks was hurt and the damage to people's houses was real bad. You was real lucky, bein' so close to the water and all."

"Anything we can do to help?" Emerson asked.

The fireman continued talking over Emerson's question. "Yessir, I sure am surprised you fared the hurricane as well as you did. I'd call it a durn site miracle."

Tom looked at Emerson then at the fireman. The fireman couldn't hear Emerson, but Tom could. That was an enlightening dose of reality for Tom. *Well*, he thought to himself, *it's clear that I am either crazier than a rabid skunk or in the middle of a miracle.*

"Yessir," the fireman continued. "I'd say you was one lucky man."

"Sometimes God's grace appears as crazy as a trapped fox," Emerson said.

"I'll say," Tom said, answering both comments. He looked over his property proudly and said, "God has been very good to to us."

"Us?" the fireman asked. Ain't you here all by yurself?"

"Just me and my bicycle, Emerson."

"Pleased to meet you," Emerson said politely.

"Well—you know—people's what I meant," the fireman replied over Emerson's unheard comment.

"I sure would be willing to help out. I'm a good fixer." Tom said, smiling, now understanding Emerson's sense of humor.

"That's awful nice of you," the fireman said. "You can volunteer down to the Baptist church. I do know we need blankets and canned goods if you got any."

Chapter Twelve

"I've got a great idea," Tom said as he searched through his house for blankets. "I'm going to make some gifts for people. . . something that will give them back their faith. It's very easy to lose it when you're in a crisis."

"You should know," Emerson said.

"Yep, been in one kind of crisis or another most of my life."

"I've got an idea." Emerson added. "I can help with your faith gift."

"How are you going to help?"

"I'll volunteer the metal from my fenders."

"For what?"

"I don't know—an inspirational gift of some kind—a trinket. You know."

"A cross. I'll cut hundreds of small crosses out of your fenders and we'll give them to the church."

"Great idea!"

So Tom carefully removed the fenders from Emerson's frame. Then with a large hammer and a big anvil that belonged to his grandfather, he pounded and hammered and finally flattened out the front fender. Then he tried to cut the metal with metal shears, but it didn't work. The metal was too thick, so he used a hack saw. After a full day of sawing and six dull saw blades. he was done—spent and tired with bloody knuckles.

"I don't think I can make anymore," he said.

"The fewer there are the more valuable they will be," Emerson said. "They will be like manna, long awaited spiritual nourishment."

So Tom drilled a hole at the top of each cross and threaded a neck chain through the hole. Then he put them in an old sewing basket. "Who should I say these are from?" he asked.

"God knows." Emerson said cleverly.

"I'll just put a "T" for Tom."

"Make it lower case."

"Like this?" Tom drew: ✝

"I think that'll be fine," Emerson said, smiling from sprocket to sprocket.

Tom found blankets from a hundred years of his family. Many had holes carefully made by generations of moths, frayed edges like out-of-focus photographs but good enough for the cold winter nights.

The church was grateful to receive the pile of blankets yet asked that "the bicycle" be left outdoors.

"Emerson's no bicycle," Tom said. "He's a real live angel."

"Still. . ." the church secretary replied, rolling her eyes condescendingly.

After Tom placed the blankets on the piles of other blankets and lifted Emerson's kickstand to leave, Emerson said,

"How many crosses did you leave?"

"Only twelve." Tom said sadly

"Uhm," Emerson said. "That's a good number."

On the way home Tom stopped to help three men who were replacing a large window in the grocery store. Then Mr. Cooper at the hardware emporium needed help dragging chairs out onto the porch. Tom smiled at the sheriff and bid him, "Good afternoon, constable."

"D'ya see the looks on their faces?" he asked Emerson.

"Disbelief—absolute, raw disbelief!"

They rode off, Tom whistling.

"Did you know that kind thoughts about helping other people come from your heart, not your head," Emerson said.

"How do you think from an organ that pumps blood?"

"That's hard to understand, isn't it? But your heart is the center of your spiritual being. What difference does it make that it pumps blood? After all, the brain is just a mass of grey matter. What makes you think that it is the only place for thought?"

"Because smart people are called 'brains'."

"Are dumb people called 'hearts'?"

"Never heard that." Tom said.

"The feeling you got from giving those blankets to people who really needed them comes from your heart. The feelings that drove you to cut twelve crosses came from your heart. The story of your life is the story of the journey of your heart. It is also the story of the long and mysterious pursuit of your heart by the God who knows you truly and loves you deeply."

Tom whistled some more.

Chapter Thirteen

And so life was good to Tom (and Emerson).
Tom never fixed the broken windows in the
breezeway. He liked the fresh air, so they
remained as a monument to his rebirth. His
driveway became a walkway where children
brought their injured bicycles so Tom and
Emerson could fix them. They never charged
money and the feeling of returning life to injured
bikes and sad children was as great to Tom and
Emerson as the feeling that autumn day that
Tom discovered God in his heart.

They rode the flats whenever they could, especially in the middle of the night, Tom pedaling as hard as he could, unable to see anything. "Blind faith," he said, racing through the night, knowing indisputably that God was good. And God was happy with Tom. He had found his purpose.

So when Tom became ill, he knew his life was full, and he was ready for his next journey.

Chapter Fourteen

It was quiet in the bedroom. Tom's eyes slowly scanned the room, recognizing images from past dimensions . . . his grandparents, the fox, and smiling faces of children. Charlie, the minister, and his wife Helen, had just finished singing Here I am Lord. Tom's son, Bill, had arrived to pay his respects to his father. A surprising sadness had enveloped him. It started in his head and traveled to his throat, then to his heart. He wished he knew his father better. Emerson leaned compassionately against the bed.

"Dad, are you sure I can't put this bicycle out in the garage?"

"No thank you, Bill," Tom said, putting his hand on Bill's and reaching his other hand out, holding Emerson by the handlebars. Then he looked hard at his reflection in Emerson's chrome. He saw peace and happiness in a blinding flash of light. It was time.

"Here I am, Lord," he said ever so quietly. His was a welcome soul, like a soldier home from the wars. . . the return of a prodigal son.

After the funeral home had removed Tom's body and everyone had left the old house on the water, only Bill remained in the bedroom. He sat quietly in a chair, his elbows on his knees, looking around the room: the bed sagging like an old mare, the broken dresser, a picture of Tom's grandmother, Emerson leaning silently against the bed.

"Tom usually kept me in the garage when he was your age," Emerson said.

Bill quickly turned around. He had thought he was alone and a sense of comfort filled his heart.

Epilog

And still on certain warm summer's nights when the tide is dead low like a sink hole in the desert and the wind is nil; the owls pause from their haunting refrain, racoons tilt their heads, coyotes curiously search the stary sky, and certain people report that they heard a far off call from the flats. It said, "Libertadis, Strongalotis et Bravelaris."

> *"If you have faith as a mustard seed . . .*
> *nothing will be impossible for you."*
> Matthew 17:20

HOW YOU CAN HELP

If you have been moved by this book and would like others to share in its message, there are a number of ways you can help.

The publishing industry has changed immensely over the past two years. Certain *uncertain* sages predict the end of the tangible book, as you and I know it. People will sit in front of their (video) fireplace with a laptop computer or Kindle. My how that distresses me! How will I underline? How will I make margin notes? So today it takes more than simply one publisher to make a book sell well. It takes a publisher, a web site, blogs, links, Myspace, author appearances, and friends telling friends. . .mostly friends.

So what can you do?

1. Tell everyone you know about Emerson. Tell them the book is available

direct from their local bookstore, online or from the publisher at: books@christiandevotions.us.

2. You and your friends are encouraged to blog on the Emerson web site, which is: http:// emersonthemagnificent.home.comcast.net These blogs go to book reviewers like New York Times, etc.

3. Write a book review for your local paper, or a web site that you frequent.

4. Talk to a friend at a local radio show to have me on as a guest.

5. If you own a retail business, consider putting a display of these books on your counter to resell to customers.

6. Talk, talk, talk, talk. In today's world, word-of-mouth rocks!

I thank you.

Dwight Ritter, Cape Cod, 2009

ACKNOWLEDGEMENTS

Cape Cod, Massachusetts. 1969. My grandfather died. My wife, JoAnn, and I found ourselves with a second home to care for. We lived an hour away, on the outskirts of Boston. I was a freelance writer and graphic artist, struggling to make ends meet. We drove down here to clean out the house and get it ready for renting. My job was the garage. I'll never forget opening the large garage doors like blinders on a working mule. The garage seemed to exhale. Dust, and chickadees drifted out. Inside was his car covered with dust, an old push lawn mower, garden tools. . .and my old red bicycle. The one I rode every summer of my life when I played down here. I dusted it off and pumped some air in the tires and rode it down to the beach. The tide was low and I sat in the sand with the bicycle laying down beside me (no kickstand). That is when I named the bike Emerson. That is when this story started.

I wrote and illustrated the first draft two years later. It was not a book about faith or God. . .or anything, just lyrical words and clever illustrations. No publishers were interested because there was no "heart" to the

77

story. Probably because I was not a believer in anything spiritual, that was for others. . .the poor, sick and unfortunate. So Emerson sat in my bookshelf for another 30 years.

Then, due to a number of personal episodes in my life, I had to reach out. . .reach out to someone/something who could help. How hard it was for me to seek and believe in an invisible, silent God.

My wife and I moved into my grandfather's house and sought comfort in a local Christian church. Our lives changed like summer to winter.

Not long ago, a writer friend of mine, Henry Scammel, happened to see my 1971 hand written and illustrated version of Emerson the Magnificent. He suggested I rewrite it. Make it spiritual, not commercial. It became a story about how hard God works to get our attention, and how stupid we are in not hearing Him. As I struggled with the rewrite and new illustrations, key people got involved; Jane Wallbrown, Doug Scalise, Pat Lindquist and my wife JoAnn. Their input shaped the book.

Then I was fortunate enough to have Diana Flegal from the Hartline Literary Agency agree to represent me and the book. Her tireless commitment to Emerson and endless encouragement to me has carried this small idea of faith. . .because of her faith. Then Eddie Jones got involved and here we are.

And throughout this convoluted process my wife JoAnn hung in there, coming up with ideas, criticisms but mostly love. Her input has always been the best. . .the most thoughtout, the cleverest, the gentlest. She remains so important, so creative, so supportive, so brave. See her art career on http://joannritterfineart. com.

"Why is God doing all this?" Tom asked.

"Because He loves you, and you are part of His special plan. God's been reaching out to you for as long I can remember."

"For as long as I first heard your voice?" Tom asked.

"Probably. And you've been trying to make sense out of it. God doesn't make sense to us."

Printed in the United States
219143BV00001B/5/P